WATCHING FOR DOLPHINS

Also by David Constantine

German Short Stories 2 [editor and part-translator],
Penguin Parallel Texts (1976)

*The Significance of Locality in the Poetry
of Friedrich Hölderlin* (MHRA, 1979)

A Brightness to Cast Shadows (Bloodaxe Books, 1980)

Talitha Cumi [with Noel Connor, Barry Hirst & Rodney Pybus]
(Bloodaxe Books, 1983)

David Constantine

WATCHING FOR DOLPHINS

BLOODAXE BOOKS

ISBN: 0 906427 54 1

First published 1983 by
Bloodaxe Books Ltd,
P.O. Box 1SN,
Newcastle upon Tyne NE99 1SN.

Bloodaxe Books Ltd acknowledges
the financial assistance of Northern Arts.

Typesetting & cover printing by
Tyneside Free Press Workshop Ltd, Newcastle upon Tyne.

Printed in Great Britain by
Unwin Brothers Ltd, Old Woking, Surrey.

For Mary-Ann and Simon

Acknowledgements

Acknowledgements are due to the editors of the following publications in which some of these poems have appeared: *Argo*, *Here Now*, *The Literary Review*, *New Statesman*, *PN Review*, *Poetry Durham*, *Poetry Review* and *The Times Literary Supplement*.

'Bracken', 'Watching for Dolphins' and the poems from *Talitha Cumi* were broadcast on *Poetry Now* (BBC Radio 3). The Homeric 'Hymn to Demeter' was broadcast in a special programme produced for BBC Radio 3 by Fraser Steel, with music by Nigel Osborne.

David Constantine's *Talitha Cumi* sequence appears in Noel Connor's poet-artist collaboration *Talitha Cumi* (Bloodaxe Books, 1983), with drawings by Barry Hirst. This is a collaboration between two artists and two poets, their collective response to the story of Jairus's daughter, the young girl whom Jesus raised from the dead with the words *'Talitha cumi'*—or, 'Little girl, awake.'

The *Journey* cycle of poems appeared in Neil Astley's anthology *Ten North-East Poets* (Bloodaxe Books, 1980). 'The Drowned' was published in David Constantine's first collection *A Brightness to Cast Shadows* (Bloodaxe Books, 1980) and is reprinted here as it has since become part of the sequence *Islands*.

Contents

Mary Magdalene and the Sun

Hugging her breasts, waiting in a hard garden
For Sun, the climber, to come over the hill,
Disconsolate, the whore Mary Magdalene,
She of the long hair. But Sun meanwhile,

Scaling inch by inch the steep other side,
At last got a grip with his fingers on the rim
And hoisted himself up. She saw the spikes of his head,
His brow, then his brazen face. So after his swim

Leander's fingers appeared on Hero's sill
And he hauled himself inside, naked and salt
And grinning. She closed her eyes and let him feel
Her open face, uncrossed her arms and felt

Him warm her breasts and throat. Thereupon a cock
Crowed once, very red. And something came and stood
Between her and the Sun, something cold, and 'Look,'
It moaned. And there, casting a shadow, naked

And bled white was the nailed man, he whose
Blessing arms they fixed on a beam, and he crouched
There gibbering of love and clutching his
Thin shoulders and begging to be touched.

He was encrusted above the eyes with black,
And maculed in the hands and feet and in his side,
And through clacking teeth he begged her to touch him,
                                        and 'Look,'
He moaned, 'at this and this that they did,'

Showing the holes. Sun, the joker, though,
Had leapfrogged him, and more cocks crowed,
And down the green hillside and through
The waking garden the waters of irrigation flowed

And plenteous happy birdsong from the air,
As Sun diminished the ghosts of fruit trees on the grass
And over the nailed man's shoulder stroked the harlot's hair
And fingered open the purple sheaths of crocuses.

Lazarus to Christ

You are forgetting, I was indeed dead
Not comatose, not sleeping, and could no more
Wish for resurrection than what we are before
Can wish for birth. I had already slid

Four days down when you hauled me back into the air.
Now they come to watch me break bread
And drink the wine, even the tactful plead
With dumb faces to be told something, and, dear,

Even you, who wept for me and of whom it is said
You know all things, what I mutter in nightmare
I believe you lie awake to overhear.
You too are curious, you too make me afraid

Of my own cold heart. However I wash
I cannot get the foist out of my flesh.

Christ to Lazarus

They faltered when we came there and I knew very well
They were already leaving me. Not one
Among your mourners had any stomach to go on,
And when they moved the stone and we could smell

Death in his lair they slid off me like cloud
And left me shining cold on the open grave
Crying for you and heaving until Death gave
And you were troubled in your mottled shroud.

They hid their eyes, they begged me let you stay,
But I was adamant, my friend. For soon
By a loving father fiercer than any moon
It will be done to me too, on the third day.

I hauled you out because I wanted to.
I never wept for anyone but you.

Candaules, Rhodope and Gyges

Gyges returned then in the ninth year
Crowned like Herakles—and heard the King confess
How *he* was prowling Love's perimeter
Certain that all within was happiness.

Dining together at a round table, who
Sat between whom that night one could not say.
Candaules and the Queen when they withdrew
Equally trailed their glances. Rhodope,

Docile to his wishes, let the candles burn
And faced him nude. But he was looking past her,
Dry in the mouth, and whispered would she turn?
Font of his happiness without demur

This too she did, smiling, almost as when
She first stood seen by one alone of men.

Minos, Daedalos and Pasiphaë

Minos himself, like any supplicant,
Came clumsily asking how it might be done.
Daedalos smiled: nothing the heart might want
Surprised him, who had Ikaros for a son.

None knew, so perfect was the counterfeit,
None among those who ran to take the bull,
Dropping bewildered from coition, in a net;
Only the King, who watched. The woman, full,

Penned what she bore in the Labyrinth to die.
It grew. They heard it roaring for the light of day,
They heard it blunder through the passages and try –
Sobbing with a human hope—another way.

They wished a slayer would come. Their normal child
Looked monstrous to the Queen. Daedalos smiled.

Priapics

1.

Godling, your mother, the smiling Aphrodite, though she loved
    Nothing so much as cock, when she had born you to
Bacchus, hid her face, and neither would own you, seeing
    What had lain covert in the divine heart of each.
Associate of Pan, impossible to clothe, they hid you in greenery,
    In gardens to threaten thieves, or you stood where roads met,
Ambushing wayfarers with their desires, and, as Priapus of
                                       Harbours,
    To you poor sailors prayed, leaving their girls.

2.

He threatened with his club impartially
    Thieves of either sex; served them alike
When, by the bed of leeks or the bed of thyme
    Caught trespassing, boy or girl turned tail.

3.

Caught fig-stealing girls departed that garden
    Only on payment of an equitable fine.
'Figs for figs,' he demanded, and the luscious part
    Of girls, the cleft and honeyed, the conducive,
The petalled-back, must cap his club. Then he arranged
    Their stolen figs coolly in a nest of vine-leaves,
And showed them out of the garden by a secret door
    Where trespassers might enter when they liked.

4.

Who are under the orbs and sceptre of King
    Prick when he says jump they jump for his
Slightest wish is their command throughout the hours of
    Daylight and darkness. Nowhere by that
Soft nose may you not lead them and to their hearts
    The way comes thence. Dead they will all
Push up the earth in molehills, the humblest
    Among them emerging as *phalli*
Impudici, while the best some flowery
    Hill will brandish as an Attis pine.

5.

How soon evasive girls walking alone and wishing
    Always to bear thus deep under their surfaces
The shadows, the quiet clouds, the shaken moon; being
    No further in than glances, than the casting,
Like dew on webs, of first love on the common courtesies,
    Have halted at him set in his covert place,
Grinning, upreared, always too soon, a hamfist,
    Botching their dreams with sense so blunt and tearing.
'Leave oil,' he says, 'leave honey, you would be wise
    To smooth me. For I am at the root and how
You grow and flower in the light and how you fume in scent
    And pass from substance to vapour, crying for love,
Crying for the happiness of your rendered soul, derives
    From me.' Some women by the way they smile, some wives,
One knows they wear the root-god for an amulet and mirror
    Skies still and every fineness of sun and stars.

'Misshapen women'

Misshapen women on the Fairhope Road Estate when the wind
    Presses upon you hurrying to the meat factory
Your breasts are not discovered through a thin chiton, nor
                           down
    The inguinal triangle do the lovely folds ripple;
And when the sun, winking behind the scrap heap, ends your
                           days
    You cannot face it smiling like caryatids,
Whom only marble burdened, for you are not fit to be
    Regarded from any angle. Only from above,
To Infinite Mercy, are your unbuttonable forms and your
    Poor mouths not an eyesore, and in an interlude
When no sun plays and no sarcastic wind He may drizzle
    Some charity upon you from a grey heaven.

The Door

Yes, that is the door and behind it they live,
But not grossly as we do. Through a fine sieve
Their people pass the incoming air. They are said
To circulate thoughtfully in walled gardens, the aged –
And they live long—wheeling in chairs. They exchange
Nothing but traditional courtesies. Most strange
However is their manner of dying, for they know the hour,
When it comes, as old elephants do. They devour
Their usual breakfast of plovers' eggs and rise
Then or are lifted by the janitors and without goodbyes
They step or are borne aloft through that door there –
And thus they end. For of course meeting the air,
The air we breathe, they perish instantly,
They go all into dust, into dead dust, and Stanley,
The Sweeper, comes with his brush and shovel and little cart
And sweeps them up and shovels them not apart
But into one black plastic bag with dimps, dog-shit
And all our common dirt. But this they intend and it
Signals their gracious willingness to reside
In the poor heart of life, once they have died.

Progress

In June, when Labour sweats, their char-à-banc
Comes nosing through the butterflies along
Forgotten green roads. The eternal Quinn
Walks the aisle among them back and forth with gin
And little chocolates from Padua. Some roar
The old songs and some in accompaniment snore.
Others have died. Their purpose in these parts
Is to inspect the farms. Tables and charts
Such as fix Easter fix their itinerary
Yet perhaps none, save Topham driving, of all their company
Knows, having arrived, whether this year Wiltshire
Or Westmorland receives them. Still, they enquire
In Latin after the yields of fields and the condition of fences,
Of hinds and swine, the increase, or whether pestilences
And civil strife have taken many off
And what the knacker gave. Ale and snuff
Outside the byre go round. They slap a cow,
A wife, and from the fob, with a free hand, throw
Pecks of advice, till Topham's ancient horn
Calls them away. Departing they have drawn
On summer evenings white inmates to
The workhouse bars in glee, but who
Has seen, uncrazed, unblinded, on Gibbet Hill
The singers tumble from their car pell-mell
Snorting to piss? Topham and Quinn decide
Among the rest who sleep and who have died
And sit the latter grinning in a row
Against a gate, by seniority; then stow
The quick, relieved, with trailing cummerbunds
And flapping spats, back in. Polite Quinn stands
Smiling upon them in a queer blue light
Such as flickers over marshes when the farts ignite.

Sad Ends

Be assured: we shall not linger for ever thus.
Conclusive death will come to all of us.
Many of our kind make sad ends,
Macabre, pathetic, even among friends
Eternally risible. Poor Tusker, full,
Dropped from the windy tiles and broke his skull
As we climbed to Common Room; our loving cup,
The horn of an auroch, carelessly raised up
Stabbed harmless Lamb; and Molineux,
Surprised by his servant and modestly clapping to
Burke's *Cornucopia Pornographica*,
Died with a sudden shout. Many are
And various the ways to Hades. At Michaelmas
I woke to find myself in utter darkness
In our library's fundament. Nobody came. Who comes
Indeed but once in a blue moon after the tomes
That interest me? Alone in the labyrinth of learning,
Cold and alone in the very sump of it and hearing
Worms gnawing my knowledge, on all fours
Crawling hither and thither in the dust for hours
Feeling for exit, I thought of someone's
Pleasure on finding me as a heap of bones
Centuries hence, some bold follower
After me in the mines of erudition or
Some paid inspector of our cloacal tracts.
O Crusius, saint of scholars, to whom such facts
As the angle of declension of the left testicle
In ancient statuary were dear, if possible
Let me get quicker below than via starvation
And, if it may be, let my passing on
Not be too foolish or indecent. May I,
Asleep, be smitten by something heavy,
Say Crowe on *Haggai* or Farthing on God's love,
Falling mercifully from a shelf above.
Let me not, ending, cause merely one more snort
Of merriment among the empurpled over their port.

'Pity the drunks'

Pity the drunks in this late April snow.
They drank their hats and coats a week ago.
They touched the sun, they tapped the melting ground,
In public parks we saw them sitting round
The merry campfire of a cider jar
Upon a crocus cloth. Alas, some are
Already stiff in mortuaries who were
Seduced by Spring to go from here to there,
Putting their best foot forward on the road
To Walkden, Camberwell or Leeds. It snowed.
It met them waiting at the roundabout.
They had no hats and coats to keep it out.
They did a lap or two, they caught a cough.
They did another lap and shuffled off.

Boy finds tramp dead

But for your comfort, child, who found him curled
With crizzled cheeks, his hands in his own ice,
Among the trapped dead birds and scraps of girls,

His spectacles and broken teeth put by
Along the window with a pile of pence,
Remember this man was the son of nobody,

Father, brother, husband, lover, friend
Of nobody, and so by dying alone
With rats hurt nobody. Perhaps he joined

And mended easily with death between
Newspaper sheets in drink and did not wake
Too soon, at midnight, crying to sleep again,

Alive and hung on cold, beyond the embrace
Of morning, the warm-handed. He was pressed
Together when you found him, child, but names

Had left his lips of wicked men released
Quickly in sunlight and of one who baked
Asleep inside a kiln and many at rest

With cancer in the casual ward or knocked
Under fast wheels. These he conjured with
To Christ as instances of mercy, being racked

Himself on boards beside a prolapsed hearth.
His vermin died. The morning's broken glass
And brightening air could not pick up his breath.

Little by little everything in him froze,
Everything stopped: the blood in the heart's ways,
The spittle in his mouth, his tongue, his voice.

Elegy

We hear you spoken of as a dead man
And where you were there is new growth of obituaries.
Someone has met an eyewitness from Darlington –
A liar, it is true. We had thought this was
Only the interruption of one of your stories

And you were working slowly on a smoke
And, tilting your indoor trilby, would appear
Through clouds soon and would broach
Your silence waiting like an untouched beer
For a man back from the gents. Remember the bloke

So bent with *arthuritis* that for his wake
They tied him to a board and in the small hours
Some joker cut his cords and, with a creak,
He sat up grinning? In a digger's jaws
Rising in a shroud of snow at bitter daybreak

You cleared a building-site; the mortuary men,
Summoned to shift you, dewy, from the road,
Have brought their breakfasts up and dropped their load
When you opened an eye. Time and again
From under newspaper we fetched you in,

A foetal stiff. Around the cup you set
Your fingers like a broken basket
And thawing your nose in tea began to tell
The story of a man from Motherwell
Who swallowed three hundred goldfish for a bet

And lived. You lived the part: the Indian doctor
Offering to amputate; nice Ronnie Kray
Visiting his mam; Lord Londonderry
Addressing your father like the man next door.
You hooked yourself a stooge when necessary.

If the liar from Darlington was right then now
The devil is leaning on his fork and you
Are keeping him waiting while you toast your bum
And roll a smoke for what is still to come
About a man you met in Eccles who...

'Many meanwhile'

Many meanwhile are turning on cruel wheels
In the pit of indifference fretting to engender fires
And only bruise and ever from the hub fall as flesh falls
From the bone and gnaw in the night on a shroud of fears.

Under the wheels, under the crosses of stars stretched out
On gaps of darkness they cover themselves and try
With a little rod to strike life that will root
And long on the sun's axis to turn securely.

Closing in sleep under one mantle, in the ears
Of sleep our breathing quieter than a murmur of sea in shells,
We think of them under their draughty lattice of stars
And dust going helter-skelter round the stuck poles.

Swans

Not many see the white swans.
Vagrants at road-ends have
Or, waiting for shift-end,
Machine-minders staring
At dereliction through the blank panes.

Not many hear them. Soiled
Drunks have whom the cold wakes
Early lying curled;
Or, nearly sleeping, the innocent
Lovers. After birdsong

That is the kindest light.
Through silver grey, through rose
Across our malignant city
The heavy birds strain
In this season, about this hour

Little above roof-tops
Rapid, whistling, intent,
Steadily clouting the air.
Pity them should they flag
For where is there a meadow

Or any habitable water
And where, landing or falling,
When the day hardens and we
Come down the roads will they
Avoid our fatal notice?

Watching for Dolphins

In the summer months on every crossing to Piraeus
One noticed that certain passengers soon rose
From seats in the packed saloon and with serious
Looks and no acknowledgement of a common purpose
Passed forward through the small door into the bows
To watch for dolphins. One saw them lose

Every other wish. Even the lovers
Turned their desires on the sea, and a fat man
Hung with equipment to photograph the occasion
Stared like a saint, through sad bi-focals; others,
Hopeless themselves, looked to the children for they
Would see dolphins if anyone would. Day after day

Or on their last opportunity all gazed
Undecided whether a flat calm were favourable
Or a sea the sun and the wind between them raised
To a likeness of dolphins. Were gulls a sign, that fell
Screeching from the sky or over an unremarkable place
Sat in a silent school? Every face

After its character implored the sea.
All, unaccustomed, wanted epiphany,
Praying the sky would clang and the abused Aegean
Reverberate with cymbal, gong and drum.
We could not imagine more prayer, and had they then
On the waves, on the climax of our longing come

Smiling, snub-nosed, domed like satyrs, oh
We should have laughed and lifted the children up
Stranger to stranger, pointing how with a leap
They left their element, three or four times, centred
On grace, and heavily and warm re-entered,
Looping the keel. We should have felt them go

Further and further into the deep parts. But soon
We were among the great tankers, under their chains
In black water. We had not seen the dolphins
But woke, blinking. Eyes cast down
With no admission of disappointment the company
Dispersed and prepared to land in the city.

ISLANDS

1. Bracken

There were sheep then, they pastured on the little islands,
We took them there by boat. But the grass has gone
And the fold my father's father built with his bare hands
Here at high water has also gone. One by one
All his fields have gone under the ferns again
And now it is hard for you to see how it was then.

Bitter, unharvested, deeper than children,
The ferns rise from high water over the wall.
The fields drown; the swinging gate is fallen
And ferns break round the posts that stand as tall
As men. But from the spring you climbed this way
After the spilling water-carts on a hot day.

You would not think we had any open ground,
But we did. We called it Plains. There was space
For all the island to be sitting round
Watching the tennis or the cricket. Our playing-place
Has gone the way of the fields and I shouldn't know
Where to look for the pitch and the court now.

Sunk flourishing in depths of bitter green
The little islands are lost to us already.
We watch from boats the rats going hungry between
Waste and waste. Remember for our sakes quickly
Where the sweet water places were and when
And by whom the fields were first rid of their bracken.

Sometimes in summer we made ourselves a bed
Under the ferns, where we should never be found,
And looked up through the lovely green at the sky and said
That we were at the bottom of the sea and drowned.
I believe sometimes we slept, but the afternoon
When we woke again was still no further gone.

We lie on the harbour wall and peering down
Where the wrack heaves and hideous claws feel
After food, we see the clouds that do not drown
In pathless water with all of our things lost but sail
Untouched through the coral and the salt flowers
Through the places of this island that once were ours.

2.

At blown cockcrow, hearing the driven sea,
You remember the rattling sash, starlight
Surviving faintly on the looking-glass
And the islands troubled with a ceaseless crying.

Scheria, kind to strangers, wept for her ship
Sunk by God unjustly; for the *Schiller*'s
More than three hundred souls there were many in
Two continents weeping; and everywhere

For the sailors of our wars, numberless
Mothers' sons who have rolled in without faces.
Indifferent Hermes conducted them all.
The sea turns and its creatures hunger. Soon

Everything lies under the mercy of day.
The surface flickers with scared pilchards.
Light, above all the light. And the sea comes,
At sunny tide-flow the plucked, the smitten sea

Comes running. The wind then, high-ridden by
One nonchalant gull, batters the opening
Eyes of the sun with water. Far-reaching,
Iridescent, the white surf comes and comes.

Children are playing under a rainbow
On Pool Green; or behind Innisvouls,
Delighted in a rocking boat, they stand
Outstaring the ancient quizziness of seals.

3.

Our child when we came looking and calling after her
And had come through marram and sea-holly to the dunes' crest
When we stood crushing in our fingers plucked samphire
Looking still further and calling and saw her at last

She was remote and small on an almost island
And turned away, at tide-flow, but our fear was less
Of the sea already parting the cord of sand
Than that she was so small and averted from us.

We ran heavily, the white sand sank us in,
But through the neck of the place stole then like bird-stalkers
Over the flat wrack that popped and stank in the sun
Towards her kneeling before big granite chairs

Gently stroking for shells. When she turned and looked up
And showed us wordless in her palm the fissured cowrie
The spiralling white horn of wentletrap
And scallops smaller than her smallest nail then we

With our looks put upon her the fear of death
And the ownership of love. Between our tall shadows
She walked to the safe beach down the snake path
Already sunk over ankles in warm shallows.

Gratefully then the weed rose in the sunny water
And swirled as it liked and flowed and the bright shell
Hoards sparkled before the thrones without her
Who stood between us watching, waiting for tide-fall.

4. The Drowned

Flat calm. The ships have gone.
By moonlight and by daylight one by one
Into a different world the drowned men rise
But cannot claw the sleep out of their eyes.
None such can know the bigger light from the less
Nor taste even the salt. Their heaviness
By no means may be leavened. Now they live
As timbers do where shipworms thrive
Only in what they feed. Strange things engross
The little galleries of thought after the loss
Of breath. The white clouds pass, but still
The drowned increase upon the senses till
The moon delivers them. On islands then
Seeing the lovely daylight watchful men
Come down and haul these burdens from the waves
And slowly cart them home and dig them graves.

5.

The trees here, though the wind leave off, never unbend.
Likewise when he sat the stick retained
The shape of the sixty years he had limped and leaned.
He would haul from under the bed with the crook-end

His bundle of photographs and the soldier's pay-book,
The usual service medals and a card or two in silk.
The marriage bed was draped to the floor like a catafalque
And he hauled the War from under it. And when he spoke

Of the craters at Ypres he used the pool on Pool Green
As measure, and the island's entanglement of brambles when
He spoke of the wire. He rose, drinking gin,
Massive, straighter than his stick, and boys were shown

At the hoisting of his trouser up the sunless calf
A place that shrank like Lazarus from being raised,
A flesh the iron seemed only lately to have bruised.
And if one, being bidden and not in disbelief,

Put in the hand to prove him right who bet
That he was past hurt there—probing appalled
In that still weeping place the fingers rolled
Wondering between them an angle of iron grit.

For year by year his flesh, till he was dead,
Evicted its shrapnel, as the living ground
Puts out for the Parson or the Schoolmaster to find,
Scouring at leisure, another arrow head.

6. Spring Tide

The summer moon was terrible. It beamed
Like Christ on Lazarus. Nobody now,
In daylight, can distinguish what he dreamed
And what he saw, in night-clothes at the window.

It was like All Souls when everything lost
And the smothered dead struggle to rise. Around
Midnight the moon hauled hand over fist
And sheet by sheet the waters were unwound.

But nothing was recovered. Still the sand,
That we saw white and phosphorescent, levels
The slopes and pleasant laps of land
And stops the doorways and the fires and wells.

The curlews cried like springs starting to run.
Then sleep began to fill us and we felt
A weeping rise and flow. Now in the sun
The sea is brimful and our cheeks are wet and salt.

7.

Sheer nowhere: the land
Ends, the rocks pile dumbly where they fell,
And hold for any life nearer to ours than lichen
There is none; the useful
Wood of wrecks whitens beyond our reach.

Rain passes, rain on the sea, and sweetens
With all its copious fall
By not one measurable jot the expanse of salt.
Clinging to islands we
Camping with our dead around a sunken plain

Such as we are, late on,
Want above all things passage to one another,
Aid and the sharing of wells
And not to swell our bitterness beyond
The normal allocation of tears.

JOURNEY

1.

Someone at least reading about beauty in a room
Above the city has turned from the lamp once having heard
Her step behind him on the creaking board and until
Morning then and until, close in the eaves, birds woke
He was allowed to lie on the narrow bed with her
Under the maps that papered the sloped ceiling
Embracing her freely and planning with her journeys.

2. Locus Amoenus

One read of the place where the covert mound rose
    Flanked by slopes, and clear water
Issued below for thirst and the excited mind
    And the senses equally were delighted.
One read of that pleasant place in the writers of pastoral
    And imagined its charms scattered over an earth
Less than so beautiful, and thinking never to come there
    Did: and found it surpassed their praises.

3. Musée du Louvre

These courtiers in a wood have come upon her
Rising before them moonlike in a clearing.
She strikes their eyes, their hands are all upraised
At the light she sheds upon them from her scallop.
Far inland henceforth, deep in the heart's covert,
Closing their eyes they will always hear the sea.

4. Musée Rodin

They saw the figures of Fugitive Love and supposed them
    Wrought to the condition of subtility
By one another's hands: she streams away
    And the soul may be seen, playing upon her limbs.
The hotel bed was bordered with a mirror
    Where they reviewed those figures, curious
What novel disposition of themselves
    Would lend their evanescence form.

5. Chartres and Avignon

One could not look through it nor did the light
    From outside enter as light of day
But passed inward in the form of a persuasion
    That love hungers and will be filled by
No dexterity. That was the window of Mary,
    Of post coitum tristis. Waking
In Avignon he saw her beside him sleeping with
    The sheet thrown off, arms and throat
Already burned from travelling. The dirty pane
    Showed a blueness under which the town
With sprinkled gutters foretasted the dust
    And thin shade under walls at noon.

6. Gothic or Classical

Reading that in the depiction of the female body
North and south of the Alps there were two traditions
By stages night after night in disreputable hotels
North and south of the Alps he examined whether
She approached more nearly the Gothic or the Classical
Bearing in mind from Paris a certain Venus
As far as Florence where a lascivious Eve
Displayed her teeth-marks in the bitten apple.

7.

The mind then seems to become the burning point
    Of the other senses, when by day
Arches are seen and one's delight converges
    At their tips and down the aisles, and when
In darkness are corresponded all parts having stiffness
    Actual or potential, likewise
All declivities and entrances and more are devised
    And the mind then is the glass, burning.

8. Rodin

Upon his dictum 'Dessiner c'est connaître'
    Gossip put a lewd connotation
Saying that master of the essence and forms of women
    Entered the place his pencil had depicted.
Oh do not leave it to gossip lewdly to imply
    Our certainty that through the foolish penis
Exact and loving knowledge comes. To that point
    The cognizance of all the senses runs.

9. Renoir

He answered: 'With my penis.' Let us not
    Imagining the inconveniences of palette and easel
And dismissing Bullhead as an unmanageable tool
    Jump to the conclusion that he meant it figuratively.

Bluebells

But then her name, coming to her averted
And more than waist-deep in the ground's embrace,
How queer it sounded, like screaming swallows,
Like bats hurting her ears. Still, she turned

And lifted her face to the rim of beech-light
And the leaf-sieved sky. And again her name
Came down the slopes to her, tugging like grief
With little cries. So she was drawn. The blue ground

Let go of her in a white furrow and where
She had entered at the horseshoe's opening
Now she began in earnest her long haul
Against the streams, ascending slowly by

Degrees of blue under the cavernous light,
A floppy corpse of flowers on her left arm
With midnight hair, with blue dark thoughts, with white
Uprooted feet. Standing in the shallows,

Black to the waist, cradling the lolling doll,
She had no sight nor sound of her lost name.
Her bluebell lips, smiling at nobody,
Clouded the cold air with a breath of roots.

Autumn Lady's Tresses

In late summer the Lady's Tresses
Spiral to light leafless and stand
Almost as bare rods. But flowers
Proceed upwards by an upbraiding or as
When the wind frays
The scything edge of a wave. Thyrsus,
Snake of ivy. Flowers
Without energy of colour, at the least remove
From the stem's green. Torch-flower,
Faintlight, but prized by finders
As much as wentletraps
The white unicorn
The winding stairway shell.

Autumn Crocuses

The naked boys, entering the light,
Their root-whiteness suffuses upwards with a colour. Then,
So long as they hold the sun's eye,
Light through and through and barely tethered,
They stand hovering. They die
When they empty of sun, sleeves
Of their life lie on the soil crumpling.

Sunflowers

Stems wrist-thick,
A pulse of plant-blood;
Faces puffing like the four winds,
A hot light. Sunflowers in the days
When they wear the aureole of power,
The licks of flame,
They lap furiously at the sun
With rasping lion-tongue leaves. But they die
As big men do whose bodies the life finds heavy, they loll
And blacken like the crucified. At evening
You will hear them in the garden flapping their rags
Groaning to fall from the fences
Flat over the grass.

Tree in the Sun

This morning the tree shed
Leaves. There wasn't a breath of wind, not
A leaf stirred on the stem
But fell for an hour or more
After the frost last night the tree stood in the sun
And the leaves fell, there wasn't a moment
When any less than hundreds were falling and neither torn
From where they held nor in their fall
By the least wind deflected as when a day falls still
And the sky silently snows so they
Were shed but it was in the sun
They fell after what cold
In the body of the tree after the withdrawal of
The lifeblood to the heart no longer held
Themselves no longer adhering when the frost relaxed
The dead leaves fell for an hour or more.
Weakened by the sun after that night
The tree shed leaves.

Song of a Woman at the Year's Turning

My children were conceived in February.
I fall in love under the hesitant light
At the year's first singing. Snowfalls
Come like reprieve, like more and quieter sleep;
Lie everywhere in a kind prevention.

Snow on my hair. It must have seemed like grey,
Like ash for a moment. But come the shining sun
Winter collapses off the necks of daffodils;
The crocuses melt, they glow like spar. My hair
I feel jet-black and jewelled with water.

What will not open, what will not rise again
The year leaves for dead. Under that law
The helpless birds sing. What will not turn
And flow now singing will be hung
Like cadavers when the flood falls. I sing.

The purple crocuses open on an iron ground.
They have a frail centre. Birds whistle
Among their frozen dead. Trembling at heart
I shall be bold as purple, unbow like daffodils
And show my wintered face to the new sun.

Atlantis
(for Lotte and Hugh Shankland)

It dies hard, the notion of a just people;
   The wish that there should have been once mutual aid
Dies very hard. Through fire, through ghastly ash and any
   Smothering weight of water still we imagine
A life courteous and joyful; see them lightly clad
   Loving the sun, the vine and the grey olive.
Over the water, from trading, they come home winged
   With sails, their guide and harbinger the white dove.

I

The sea suddenly stood up vertical, sky-high,
Bristling with the planks of their peaceful ships.
The earth roared like a bull. They said Poseidon,
Breaker of lintels, was shaking them. There was fire too
Glaring like a red eye. But the unkindest
Was of all the four elements the purest
And to breathing man his being: the air
Clagged and precipitated in cankers of pumice
And thereafter for weeks in a fine dust.
Wherever the living air was welcome now
Ash entered and the hearts of houses ceased;
Their eyes, hurt by blows, were quite extinguished;
Their mouths, agape, were stopped. Ash filled
And softly embedded household pots, shrouded
Frescoes of air-breathing dolphins. Who survived
When the sun had wept and blinked its eyesight clear
Lame in the lungs saw only dust
Lying now quiet as snow. One inch of such –
That is from nail-end to the knuckle of the thumb –
Will render infertile the fruitful, the man-nurturing earth
For perhaps ten years. To them now kneeling on rock
Who had salted no fields, burned no olive groves
And poisoned nobody's wells, there remained no rod
To sound the ells, the fathoms, the generations of ash.

II

How deep below? None of the warring nations
Had length of chain to fathom at what depth
Atlantis lay. Nobody anchored there. But then –
In the days of death by impalement or the ganch
When Christian citizens of Candia ate
The besieging Turk—with a roar, witnesses say,
Like innumerable bulls, the sea, or the earth
Under the waters, rendered up to the surface
A new island, called nowadays *Kaimeni*,
The cinder. On Santorini the common people,
Scratching a living in the old ash and pumice,
Remembered Kalliste and watched and prayed. But a scholar,
A believer in Atlantis, when the steam had thinned
Pulled out alone in a small boat. How great
Must have been his disappointment if he thought
Some glimmer of Atlantis might be vouchsafed him
(Who had done no especial wrong in wicked times)
If he hoped for some however dim intimation
Of their lost lovingkindness and wisdom: he saw
Only black smoking slag and ash, and smelled
An intimation of Christian Hell. Also
The hot sea soon uncaulked his punt and rowing
Desperately heavily for home he sank
In depths well known to be unfathomable.

Chronicle

Scabby with salt the shipwreck wondering
Upon what shore, among what manner of savages
He was tossed up, found himself received
With a courtesy near to veneration. Lies
Were ready on his tongue but he found
His rescuers, his hosts, discreet or indifferent
And asking nothing. Only once he was bathed
And dressed in clothes held by for the occasion
There was a pause, a silence, and his fear returned
Imagining sacrifice. Solemnly, deferring,
They led him into the church. The congregation
Was the island's marriageable girls. He must choose,
They said, one for his bride. Any stranger
Showing himself indignant or lascivious
Heard behind him the whetting of knives. The wise man
Walked modestly two or three times
The length of the aisle and among the girls after
The heart's true inclination made his choice.
A priest of the church married them there and then.

Next morning early with a harder courtesy
He was fetched aboard a manned ship and so
Passed back into the sea-lanes. Some thus restored
Put off the escapade, some boasted and some
Wandered thereafter for the one bride. She
According to the custom of the island was courted by the best
And if she were seen to have taken the stranger's seed
Then by the very best, and married in her third month.

The second husbands shone like full moons
In reflected sun, their stepchildren
Were called 'the strangers' and enjoyed
Love and privileges above the rest. The boys
Grew proficient with boats, eyed the horizons
And one morning departed, courting shipwreck. The girls
Excited a restlessness but themselves
Waited, knowing they were most likely to be chosen
When out of the sea one morning a salt man crawled.

Sunium

Dawns may be rose and dove-grey
Evenings blue-black like Persephone
Lovely. But the culmination at noon
At sheer midsummer
That is incomparable.

Remember the bay, the water clear
As nectar in a calyx. There the sun
Brought our perception of carnal life
To the burning point.

Then the horizons had no attraction
There was no drowsiness, we watched
And bathed and sweetened the mouth with fruit.

Where promontories embrace an arena of sea
At noon the bivalve opened
The mollusc wings
The lips.

Lasithi

Lasithi: notable for windmills. Summits are
   The petals of Lasithi and their snow
Streams underground. Ten thousand mills, sailing like toys,
   Crank it to surface into troughs. At dawn
The families come down to a lake of mist. Women
   In black unmoor and swivel the bare crosses
To feel the wind. The rods blossom and in its throat
   A well reaches for water like a man
Strangling. It mounts like birdsong then—o lovely work
   Of slowly scooping sails—it fills the reed,
The wells respire, the cisterns wait like mares and when
   In leaps, crashing like laughter, water comes,
A full wellbeing ascends and wets the walls and brims and
   Down the runnels like amusement overflows
Under the leaves, along the root-courses, and men
   Go about with hoes gently conducting it.

After the evaporation of the mist, under
   The sheer sun, under descending eagles,
Rimmed with snow, veined silvery with water and laced
   With childish flowers, the plateau works. The mills
Labour like lilies of the field, they toil and spin
   Like quivering cherry trees in one white orchard.

The Diktaean Cave

Children, attend. The myths are bloody. In this wet crack
For Mother Rhea, weary of fruitless birth, the Kouretes
Hid God the Usurper, little Zeus, from the cunning,
The child-swallowing Kronos—himself a son who for his mother,
Gaia, the Earth, weary of copulation, reaped from his father,
Vast Ouranos, the parts necessary with a jagged sickle.

The cry a hurt sky makes echoes for ever.
His fading semen splashed Heaven. Seaborn
Of the rosy froth where the unspeakable fell, our fierce
And gentle need grew. Blow out the candle. Darker
Than this and unimaginably deeper is Tartarus where grown
Zeus confined outwitted wily Kronos, having exhumed

Vigorous brothers and sisters from his guts. Zeus lived
The life of Riley then in the upper air, with clouts
Of thunder and strokes of the rod of lightning lording it;
And pressed divinity small into the bull, the swan, the eagle,
The golden dancing gnats, when tugged by Love, the immortal,
For one of the black earth's mortal sons and daughters.

A Relief of Pan

Standing behind you in the looking-glass
I saw my foolish admiration cross
Your own dispassionate appraisal of your dress.
I met your eyes, I saw you wished me gone,
I thought of that man by the Zappeion
Who likewise could not let you be in peace.

I had gone looking for a sanctuary of Pan
Along the dry Ilissos, you by the drinking-fountain
Sat eating cherries. I had gone
Looking unsuccessfully for a relief of Pan and he
Meanwhile, your gentleman of the Zappeion,
Was proffering you his member round an ilex tree.

Brother of mine, the Nymphs will not come down
To dead Ilissos, nor can you watch at home
A girl before her glass from nakedness become
Clothed like a stranger at the drinking-fountain
Nor watch her put off every ornament again
Saving a jewellery of cherries. I can,

I do. Yet I imagine being found
One day in shrubs below her window or by stairs
She might descend or shuffling after her in queues,
Eyes down, with cunning mirrors on my shoes.
I think it will amaze the officers
To learn what lady I have importuned.

Perdita

The brusqued sun returned, but milder, as
Through leaves over water, and silence too,
After the sprung lock, a clamour of birds
On the lake in the heart's forest settling.

Then nothing was between them but her bed
And that narrow. Come near to either bank
And staring neither saw when they began
At the throat the undressing very much of

The other's appearing nakedness since the eyes
Across the pause held them to their purpose
By force of looking face to face. Only
When she reached for the counterpane he saw

How bare her hand was and how thin her wrist
When she took off the covers and they stood
Shivering and unable to get breath
Beside a girl's sheets who with solemn dolls

Behind thin flowery curtains lessening
The strongest light had owned, until he backed
With pressing hands the blank door to, a room
As still as the heart pool of a forest.

TALITHA CUMI

1.

Lazarus was heavy but she, little sister,
When he spoke to her softly in the common speech
She sat up beckoned by his little finger
Puzzled to be present at so important a *levée*.

They gave her milk to drink in her usual bowl.
Her lip took a white moustache. She made
Crumbs on the counterpane thoughtfully breaking bread.

2.

Sweet breath. She amused herself
Clouding her mother's mirror and with finger-tips
Then causing her re-appearance. Light
In a black grape held between finger and thumb
This pleased her too, and squinting at the sun
To discern its heart of darkness, and on her tongue sometimes
Curiously she felt for bitterness in honey.

3.

In dreams she was trailed again through the clear void
And caused the unborn to appear
Twinned with the dead. They seemed
A poppy-head bursting slowly or
The milky river of stars. They hung
Upon her when she returned
Like rime. She sat up thoughtfully
Against a hemisphere of Persephone blue
In which the comets and the little moons were vanishing.

4. Glossolalia

She sank or swam. Her father's pier of knowledge
Reached nowhere in that sea. He watched. She drowned
And surfaced, crying out and babbling in a language
High in rapid vowels, a tongue attuned

To pleading, like none he knew. The lamp held
Towards her eyes showed him himself unseen;
And pressing her cold hands he was only chilled
And could not wake her. She had lost her own

True intonation and having passed below
A surface spoke refracted. He feared that there
She had been loved at once and was missed now
And Death came pestering and questioning her,

A mistress of his tongue, and swore she lied
When she denied all knowledge of his seed.

5.

Within a month then came
Her first issue of blood. She feared
Another leaching of her strength but this
Was only the moon's small opportunity for life
Spent by her woman's body. Still
She lamented the going of her blood as though it were children.
Her heart was anxious like a linnet in a mine.

6.

O Kore with the little hurting breasts
Your elders' eyes are on you worse than mirrors.
Men waver in their looks when you put down
Your childhood one day like a doll and take
It up again the next with lavish love.
The women soon, too soon in their own lives,
All winter long lament Persephone,
Calling on God to send us a saviour,
A radiant child, they coax you out of the dark
Like pale narcissi. Returning girl
Our love of beauty and our fear of death
Oppress you worse than clouds. Look for a clearing
Ankle-deep in red anemones and pool
Your innocence with some ardent fumbling boy.

7. Chanticleer

The child's familiar whose stabbing beak
Tickled her palm for crumbs, the strutting lord
And master of a few hens in the little yard
Had never so woken her. The cock's head broke

Like bedlam through the tympanum of sleep,
Suffused, red-lappeted, with a wicked eye.
She saw him swell upon the eastern sky,
Showing the rose, the red and gold, and step

From the sea like God, crowing, splashing salt,
Turning the globe with claws. Her Chanticleer,
Her little favourite, she felt him sear
The dew away and savagely exult.

He had become a lord of thorns and a lord of spurs,
Of thorns flowering, of spurs raking his rivals
Until they streamed. There were no other pools
On the dry ground. The dew had gone and hers,

She thought, was the only charity left to the hard
Flamboyant earth and the brilliant salt sea.
Chanticleer stamped and rioted in the sun and she
Hid from him like the lidded well in the yard.

8.

Reluctant child. The family have gone
Calling for her to follow, climbing the fernhill.
Everyone has gone. But she still kneels
And strokes the shingle with her finger-tips for one
More augur, wentletrap or cowrie shell.

Mist. The familiar fernhill enters the sky.
The levels flood. The herd of tumuli,
The graveyard and the little islands
Lift from a drifting ground. The smothered sea
Creeps from oblivion in long winding bands.

Emerges. Breathes. All things become their ghosts.
The sun dissolves. But there are gaps of lightness against
A shoulder or between disappearing mounds
And dunes of the cliff-hill. Like a finger-post
High on the borders of daylight somebody stands

Singular on this island without trees
Calling a version of her name. But she is on hands and knees
Over a pool of shells and if she hears or sees
She pays him no attention. She may be sure
That more than once he will turn back for her.

The drowned are lowing in the fog. Come along,
She remembers them calling. She blinks the wet from her lashes
And sees a white sun shrinking and distending
And someone, stark as a post, more urgently beckoning.
Clutching her shells she begins the trudging paths.

Love of the Dark

We loved the rain, it bathed our minds to think of
The replenishing rain. On a morning then
The cloud had lifted and we saw the whiter
Splash of the stream at the cwm mouth and the wall

Through which the bracken trickled. Behind that dyke
Ownerless herds of fire cropped, unhousing
Little birds but leaving springs in hoofmarks and
On a craterous level above two valleys

The lake where once in a cotton grass summer
White gulls lifted quietly from the surface
And we undressed to bathe. I showed you afterwards
Blood on a stone, feathers and a bridge of bone.

Love of the dark, love of the falling silent
Of everything but the stream... We left the road
At nights, we trespassed over the properties
By the white clue of the climbing stream, by red

Lanterns of rowan. Above the stepping falls
Under the lintel of the lion-gate fold
And through a hogg-hole in the cyclopean wall
We entered our sleep like children. Hand in hand we

Ran some distance to the last skyline. The lake
Still lay in a sun- and moonlight at a time
Of the soft drifting of cotton grass or when
Ice clouded over our full crater of rain.

Moon

Under compulsion when the moon turned murderous
Coldly we walked out during the white hours
Who should have kept ourselves indoors for warmth
Asking of one another only mercy.

Sweetheart, I pleaded, under this hag moon
We must say nothing and look upon nothing.
Come in and sleep now or we shall convert
Our universe to ash and ice and stone.

Her hung and bitter face setting against me,
Look everywhere, she said, once and for all
And speak of everything and show me if you can
Some love still living under my truthful moon.

Turning to look I gave our fields to ash,
I creased the brows of hills with lines of stone,
I struck the wincing surface of our lake,
I wrinkled every stream. In silence then

Standing triumphant by the sobbing ice
I cupped my hands in trickling dust for her
Whom fever shook. Moon love, she said,
This being done how will you warm me now?

Red Figure Vase

Black where he is now who drew them, lightless
   My love, and where they are and all those
Like them, the youth and the girl, and where we
   Shall be, over the curve no sun,
No star ever rising. Black. See how they shine,
   Their fired bodies. Smiling she curves
Ascendant daylight over him to quench
   With her cone his standing torch. That done
Were they living they would sleep as we do
   Sightless, enfolded warm, on black.

VERSIONS FROM THE GREEK

'Some say nothing on earth'

Some say nothing on earth excels in beauty
Fighting men, and call incomparable the lines
Of horse or foot or ships. Let us say rather
Best is what one loves.

This among any who have ever loved
Never wanted proof. Consider Helen: she
Whom in beauty no other woman came near
Left the finest man

In Greece and followed a much worse to Troy
Across the sea and in that city forgot
Father, mother and her baby girl. For where
Cypris led her there

She followed as women will who are all
Malleable under love and easily turned.
My absent Anaktoria do not likewise
Put me from your thoughts.

For one glimpse of your lovely walk, to see
The radiance of your face again I'd give
The chariots of all Lydia and all their
Armoured fighting men.

[SAPPHO]

'Gods are not happier'

Gods are not happier than I think he
Must be who sits before you face to face
Listening closely to your every word
Beloved girl I

See how he loves to hear your laughter, my
Beloved laughing girl, it hurts my heart
When I see you I cannot speak, nothing
Comes to me to say

My tongue is tied and at the sight of you
I have the sensation of fine fire
My eyes are blinded and there is the din of
Deafness in my ears

The sweat streams down me cold, I am shaken
Through and through and look lanker than the grass
In summer. I think I cannot bear much more,
My life will fail me.

[SAPPHO]

'O Love'

O Love throned splendidly among the immortals
O goddess scheming child of Zeus the Father
Lessen I pray you my multitude of griefs
Lady if ever

Before now when I prayed to you you heard me
And harnessed your chariot and left the golden
Halls of Zeus the Father and came to me
Come to me now. For

Then your delightful sparrows on whirring wings
Brought you from heaven in a moment down
Through the middle air over the black earth
Here to me, smiling.

I saw you before me face to face, Lady.
You asked what were the things that troubled me
And what I wanted calling on you again
And what of all things

What fall of events would please best my
Impassioned heart. 'And whom shall I turn now
And lead into your love? Who is it slights
You now, my Sappho?

For she who runs from you soon will pursue you
She who refuses gifts soon she will give them
And if she does not love you soon she will
Though she wish not to.'

Come to me now therefore and deliver me
From grief and difficulty and what my heart
Wants I beg you accomplish and be at my side
In love's war, goddess.

[SAPPHO]

Three Poems

The moon has set. So have the Pleiades.
Midnight. The hours pass. I sleep alone.

* * *

The dust of Timias who was received before her wedding
    Dead into the chamber of dark Persephone;
And for whom when she died being their equal in years
    Her companions in mourning cut off locks of hair.

* * *

Dead and going below you will leave a memory
Unable to survive. For of their roses, who inhabit Pieria,
You had no share. Your soul, flying from here, in Hell
Will trail obscurely among the shadowy dead.

[SAPPHO]

Versions from the Greek Anthology

The only lovers, virgin, you will find
Among the dead, having withheld
Your pleasure from the living, lie
Bare to the bone, in dust.
[V. 85]

Night and the lamp, we took
None other into the confidence of our vows,
Swearing to love, never to leave,
Calling them to witness. Now
Those promises, he says, were written on water.
The lamp shines on him sleeping elsewhere.
[V. 8]

Pan, losing the boy Daphnis, will come,
He says, into the town with his grief.
Because Daphnis is dead the herds will want a master,
The mountains music and the wild animals a hunter.
The god Pan will be among townspeople,
Goat-footed, lamentable.
[VII. 535]

You only waste your garlands and the myrrh
On tombstones; do not feed the pyre.
Bestow your gifts upon me living if you would.
Wine on my ashes now makes only mud.
[XI. 8]

The wine, going often between us,
Laid me to sleep at the mercy of his love.
What was put off I lay before you, Cypris,
My girlhood in the clothes sodden with perfume.
[V. 199]

'He has few hairs'

He has few hairs, only about the ears
And those are grey, and fewer remaining years
And those are sad. He has said goodbye
To the last youth. Nobody
Beckons him now but death, the one
Lover from whom there is no moving on.

[ANAKREON]

Agamemnon to Achilles

The son of Atreus, murdered Agamemnon, addressed him,
Dead Achilles, son of Peleus, ghost to ghost: 'Dying at Troy,
Far from Argos, you were fortunate, my friend. For around you,
Former charioteer lying a long corpse in the choking dust,
Our best and theirs struggled and died, all day and
Never should have desisted but God the Thunderer
Stopped us with a storm. Then we carried you out of battle
To the ships and laid you on a bed and washed
Your body clean with warm water and anointed you.

The Danaans wept for you, Achilles, gathering round,
And cut their hair. And your mother when she knew
Came out of the sea with the Nymphs who do not die
And over the sea there arose a terrible crying.
The soldiers were afraid and would have fled into the ships
Had not our Nestor, the long rememberer and frequent
Giver of good advice, restrained them saying: "Do
Not run, it is his mother and her immortal nymphs
Come to look upon the face of her dead son." The Achaeans
Recovered their courage. The daughters of the Old Man of the Sea
Dressed in the robes of unending life stood around you
Weeping, and the Nine Muses took up among them
To and fro the death-song and every soldier there was moved
By the Nine thus singing, to and fro, such singing,
And wept. For seventeen days and seventeen nights Achilles
We mourned you, men who would die themselves together
In one company with immortals, and gave you to the fire
On the eighteenth day, butchering fat sheep in sacrifice
And cattle. You burned in clothing of the gods, you were sweet
And rich with salves and honey and as you burned our bravest,
Bearing their weapons, circled the pyre in chariots and on foot,
Crying aloud. Burning like a forge when the flames had
                                        consumed you
At dawn we collected your white bones Achilles
And laid them in pure wine and oil. Your mother gave us
A golden urn, the gift, she said, of the god Dionysos,
The work of great Hephaestos. Therein we placed your bones,
Famous Achilles, together with those of Patroklos,
Son of Menoetios, who died before you. The bones of Antilochos,

Whom you loved above all others when Patroklos was dead,
We placed close by and over all we soldiers raised
A colossal mound on a high headland above
The Hellespont where the waters widen so that in our
Generation and in all generations to come
Men at sea will mark it from a great distance.'

[*Odyssey*, XXIV. 35-84]

The Hymn to Demeter

Listen. I shall recite the old story
Concerning Demeter, Our Lady of the Lovely Hair,
And Persephone, her daughter, who was good
At running, skipping, dancing and whom Aidoneus,
The Receiver of Corpses, raped whilst her
Own father, Zeus, the biggest noise among
The host in Heaven, turned his eyes, famous
For missing nothing, the other way. Golden
Demeter, whom we reap with sickles, who loads
Our laps with fruit, had let her go out of sight.

She was playing in a meadow by the streams
Of Ocean with his daughters, the Nymphs,
Whose beauty were we ever to see them
With bare breasts would dement us. She was picking flowers,
Roses, crocuses and pretty violets,
Irises and hyacinths, but for a particular flower,
A narcissus put up by Gaia, the Earth,
To please Hades, on God's say-so, for this
Outshining flower the girl, herself
Like an opening flower, reaching was caught. But any
Human being for his life-span and any god
For ever would have looked with amazement
On that flower which from the root rose to a cluster
Of a hundred blooms and their scent was such
That the wide sky above and the whole earth
And the salt waves of the sea smiled.
                                       The girl,
Breath-taken, was reaching out both hands
For Gaia's beautiful toy when the ground
That bears our footpaths there and then, in Nysa
On the plain, came open and the Lord who plucks
Us all in fistfuls, son of Kronos, many-named,
Horsedrawn rose upon her.

                         She was light.
She could not root there like the olive trees.
She fell on his scything arm like a thin sheaf
Crying in a girl's high voice to Zeus,

Her father, of all gods master, and was heard by no-one,
God or man, but only Perses' daughter,
The thin moon Hecate, listening in her cave,
Shuddered, woman for woman, and Helios,
The sun, he heard her crying for pity to
Her father Zeus. But Zeus was sitting apart
Where prayers arrive, receiving offerings, sweet
In the nostrils, from shortlived men. And he whom we
Call Lord of Millions, Receiver of Millions,
Was carting off the daughter of brother Zeus,
The blind-eye-turner, screaming. So long
As she still saw the earth and the sky where sun
And stars shine and the ebbing and flowing sea
Where fishes thrive she hoped still she
Would be let go back to her beloved mother and
Her friends and relatives in Heaven. Hope,
Though she was frightened, still comforted her. She ripped
The world with cries, from mountain-top to sea-bed.

Demeter, fruitful goddess, sickle queen,
When she heard the echoes of crying Persephone
Froze in her heart and tore from her head of hair,
Lovely as fields of corn, the coif, threw off
The cloak, of swallow blue, from her shoulders
And flew then over the dry land and over the water
In bird-shape, searching. But nobody, man
Or god, would tell her the truth, nor did
Any bird come with a true report. Nine days,
With burning torches in her hands, she wandered
The world and grieved so that she neither ate
The food of the gods nor drank their drink nor washed
Her body with water. But when dawn came
With light on the tenth day Hecate met her,
She too carrying a torch, and said:
                                    'Demeter
Who has taken away from you who give
The earth its seasons and heap our arms with gifts
Your child Persephone? I heard her crying
But what was being done to her, by whom,
I could not see. Your face is smeared with grief.'

The daughter of Rhea could not reply, but flew

At once with Hecate, bearing torches, to Helios,
The look-out for gods and men, and stood
By his horses. Demeter addressed him:
                                    'Helios
Will not you at least, if ever I
Have shown you any favour in word or deed
Now in return pity me? The daughter I bore,
My darling and beautiful child, I heard her
Suffering force and crying to thin air
But with my own eyes saw nothing. You
Look down with beams from the bright sky over all
The land and sea. Tell me then honestly
If you have seen her anywhere and who
It was who used his strength on her when she
Was out of my sight.'
                        'Demeter, Rhea's
Daughter, queen, I reverence you,
And pity you now grieving for your slim girl.
Listen to the truth: the one to blame is Zeus,
Concealed in cloud, who gave her to Hades,
Brother Death, to be enjoyed as wife below
Ground in the dark. Crying her heart out
She was taken off, black-horse-drawn. However
Neither your loud grief nor your anger
Persisting till kingdom come will help matters.
Therefore desist. She might have done much worse
Than him, Lord of the Millions of the Dead and your
Own brother, a child, like you, of father-castrating
Kronos. At the share-out in the first place
He was given his due, one third, and over those
He lives with now (the dead) he was made lord.'

Thus Helios. He called to his horses. At his shout
They hauled him rapidly away like long-
Winged birds. But the grief and the bitterness of Demeter
Were all the worse and, hating Zeus, she shunned
The meeting-places of the gods and high Olympus
And went among men instead, into their towns
And over their rich fields, for a long time, and made
Herself unlike herself in looks and no man seeing her
And no compassionate woman knew her until
She came to the house of Celeus, the wise,

Who was at that time king of scented Eleusis.

She was sitting by the roadside, nursing her grief,
By the Maiden Well, where the women of the town
Drew water, in the shade, under an olive tree.
She had the appearance of a very old woman,
A woman past childbirth and the pleasures of love.
She might have been the nurse of a king's children
Or a housekeeper in his palatial rooms.
And the daughters of Celeus, son of Eleusis,
Found her by the well when they came to draw water
And carry it home in bronze pitchers
To their father's house. The girls were as beautiful
As we think goddesses, they were like Persephone
In the flower of girlhood and called Callidice,
Cleisidice and Demo and the eldest one
Callithoë. They approached in all innocence –
For often when we see them we do not know the gods –
And asked her what family she was of
And where she was from and why one of her great age
Was avoiding the towns and the houses where women
As old as she and younger in cool rooms
Might make her welcome. She greeted them courteously:

'Your mother, whoever she is, is fortunate
To have such daughters. Since you ask I will tell you
The truth about myself. Why not? The name
My mother named me is Doso. I have come from Crete
Across the wide back of the sea against my will,
Forced to, by men. And when they beached their ships
At Thoricus the women went ashore
In a crowd, their masters with them, to make a meal
By the stern-cables. But I had no appetite
And when they were not looking I ran away
Into the dark inland and so escaped
From the men, my owners, who had crossed the sea
To sell me, got for nothing. Now I am lost
And ignorant of what country this is
And who its people are. But may the gods
Who have their home on Olympus help you to
Good husbands and by them children as men
And women in marriage wish if now, girls,

You will have pity on me and tell me whom
I can go and work for at the jobs that women
My age do. I could cradle a baby
Lovingly in my arms or keep the house
Or spread my master's bed in the sleeping-place
Or teach the women their jobs.'
                                    Callidice,
Best of the four in looks and belonging to no man,
Answered the goddess:
                    'Mother, what the gods send
We have to suffer. We are nothing to them. But listen
I will tell you the names of the men who are powerful
And honoured here, who govern the people and uphold
The city's coif of towers by wisdom,
Truth and justice. They are Triptolemus,
Dioclus, Polyxeinus, Eumolpus,
Dolichus and our father Celeus. If you went
To the wife of any one of these at home
She would not insult you, she would not turn you away,
But you would be welcome at her door for there is
Divinity in your appearance. Or,
If you will, stay here and we shall run home
And tell our mother Metaneira who,
Hearing all this, will have you come to us
And not go asking at the houses of others. We have
A boy at home, late-born, much prayed for,
Welcome when he came, on whom we dote. Were you
To be his nurse until he was a man
Our mother would reward you with such gifts
That women would envy you.'
                            To Callidice
Finishing speaking Demeter bowed. They filled
Their shining pitchers and full of happiness
They hurried to fetch the water home and tell
Their mother all they had heard and seen. She sent
Them back on the instant to offer the stranger
A place in their household for the rest of her days.

Like fawns and calves when they in the spring of the year
Go bounding into a new meadow and their senses
Delight in the grass so the daughters of Metaneira
Ran holding up their trailing skirts

76

Down the sunken path and from off their shoulders
The long hair lifted as bright as crocus flowers.

They found the goddess sitting by the roadside
Where they had left her, and conducted her home.
She walked behind them grieving, her head covered
And a dark cloak flapping about her feet.

Soon they arrived, and went through the portico
Of Celeus' house to where their mother sat
By a pillar, the newborn boy-child
In her lap. The girls ran to her. But the goddess
Stood on the threshold: her head reached to the lintel,
She filled the doorway with a shining light
And Metaneira when she saw her was seized
With awe and reverence and pale fear. She rose
And asked Demeter to be seated but she,
Bringer of seasons, the perfect benefactress,
Would not be seated on the bright couch and stood
Saying nothing, with eyes cast down, until Iambe,
Seeing what was best, placed a folding chair
For her and threw over it a silvery fleece.

Demeter sat, holding her veil in her hands
Before her face. She sat on the stool for a long time
Saying nothing, only grieving, and greeting no-one
With any word or gesture, but only sat
Unsmiling, taking nothing to eat or drink
But pining for her daughter, wasting over the loss of
Her beautiful child. And only Iambe,
Seeing what would help and who never lost the gift
Of pleasing the goddess, said things that made her smile
And laugh, and lightened her heart. Then Metaneira
Poured her a beaker of wine but she refused it
Saying she was not permitted to drink red wine
And asking that they mix water, barley and pennyroyal
For her instead. This Metaneira did, and gave
The potion to Demeter as she asked, and so,
Receiving it, she made the sacrament.

                                        Metaneira
After a silence was the first to speak:

'Welcome, Lady. I wish you nothing but good.
I think you are not of ordinary parentage.
Your face is delightful to look at and
Like that of a queen and law-giver
Inclines us to reverence. We who are not gods
Must submit to what they send although it be
A yoke of sorrow. Since you have come to us
I will give you what I can. Will you nurse my son
Whom the gods have given me now late in my life
After much prayer and when I had stopped hoping?
If you will bring him to the start of manhood
When your work is done I will reward you with such gifts
That you will be envied among the women.'

                                           Demeter,
Haloed with shining hair, said 'Lady
Blessings upon you likewise, and may the gods
Endow you with good. I will be, as you ask,
Your baby's nurse and bring him up, nor shall,
Through carelessness of mine, any ill come near him
Nor will he suffer pains, for against ill-wishing
And to ward off pain I have a wealth of knowledge.'

Then Metaneira was happy and handed her son to
The goddess, who hugged him close. So he,
Demophoön, child of Celeus, a good man,
And Metaneira, the loving, was nursed in the palace
And grew like an immortal not fed with food nor drinking
A mother's milk, for by day shining Demeter
Smeared his body with ambrosia as though he were
Her own son and a god and breathed upon him
Sweetly as she hugged him close. But at nights unbeknown to
His loving parents she would lay him like a coal in
The secret heart of the fire. They saw with wonder
Their child growing beyond his years and becoming
For them, mortal, like a god to look at. She would
Have given him eternal youth and eternal life
Had not Metaneira, the careful mother, wrongly
One night, anxious to see, come down. She saw
And clutched her two hands upon her heart
And screamed in fear for her beloved son and cried
Beside herself: 'My child, Demophoön, the stranger

Is burying you in the heart of the fire, alas
She has done us a terrible harm.' Demeter,
Brighter to look at than a white fire, heard
The ashen woman moaning and that dear child,
The late-comer, the mother's no longer hoped for,
She snatched with her unconsuming hands from the flames
And threw him from her down on the ground in terrible
Anger, crying: 'Humanity, what fools you are
Without foreknowledge of the good or the evil
Coming your way. O human mother, the folly
You have done will never be undone. I swear
By Styx, by the pitiless waters, and give you my word
I should have made him deathless, your dear son,
Nor would he have aged and the honour I gave him
Would have been everlasting. But now he will not elude
By any means Death and the Fates. Only this, that he
Once lay upon my knees and slept in my arms
Will be his glory and cannot be undone. In time
However, in his beautiful manhood, the sons
Of Eleusis will go to war with one another
And there will always be discord. I am Demeter
Honoured by gods and men as bringer to both
Of help and joy. But now let all your people
Build me a great temple and an altar below it
Below the city and its sheer wall, above Callichorus
Upon a rising hill. I will teach you my worship
So that afterwards piously doing as I say
You may incline me to kindness.'
                                 Then Demeter
Changed her stature and her appearance, put off
Old age, the air about her shone
With beauty, streamed with the scent of her clothes,
Her body was a bright light and her hair
Tumbled down shining upon her shoulders. The house
Filled with a brightness like that of lightning.
So she left them.
                    Metaneira could barely stand.
She remained for a long time dumb, forgetting
Even to take up her baby, her lastborn,
Who lay on the floor. He cried and cried until
He woke his sleeping sisters. They came running
And one took him up in her arms and hugged him close,

Another mended the fire, another hastened
Quietly to bring the mother away. Then all
Crowding together they bathed the kicking child
And cuddled him. But he would not be comforted
Because these nurses and maids holding him now
Were not the goddess. All night they never left off
Praying to be back in her good graces again,
All night shaking with fear. But when the morning came
They told the whole story to the ruler Celeus
As Demeter, haloed with a blinding beauty,
Had said they must. Their father assembled the people
And said they must build a temple to Demeter
And an altar, on the hillock. And they obeyed
And built it, for the goddess. And when they had done
Labouring and building the men went home again
Each to his family.

     But Demeter, the corn-golden,
Sat alone in the home they had built her
Still shunning the company of all the blessed gods
Thin in the face for grief over Persephone
Her child. And on the earth that nurtures us all
She inflicted such a year as we shall never forget,
A hungry year. The seed would not sprout in the ground
For grieving Demeter shut it. The oxen ploughed
The fields for nothing and the white barley in handfuls
Fell on the land like pebbles. She would have starved
The human race to death and the Olympians
Would have gone short of the tithes and sacrifices
Which they exact from men, had not Zeus, the canny,
Turning the matter over, sent Iris, winged
With golden light, to fetch Demeter, whose beauty
They were missing.
     Iris obeyed black Zeus
And flew quicker than rainshafts through the air
And coming to the fragrant city of Eleusis
Found Demeter alone in her temple wrapped in black
And said:
    'Lord God Almighty Zeus, absolute
In wisdom, wants you back, Demeter, where you,
Goddess, belong, among the immortals, so come
Do as he wishes.'

Iris begged her. But she,
Grief-stricken, would not obey. Then Zeus,
The eternal happiness in Heaven being troubled,
Sent down to her one after the other
All the gods, and they came in turn, calling her name
And bringing beautiful gifts and offering whatever
Favours in Heaven she cared to choose. But nothing
Moved her, and nobody, so deep-rooted now
Was her bitterness. She closed her ears to their bribes
And swore she would never set foot again on Olympus,
Their scented heaven, and never release the seed
From prison in the ground, until she saw her child
Persephone, the bright-eyed. Zeus, big noise,
Know-all, when he heard this despatched
The Killer of Argus and Bearer of the Golden Rod
To Hell, with suitable blarney there to softsoap
Brother Death and lead the chaste Persephone
Out of the dark, through the mists, into the light,
Into the company of the gods again, that Demeter,
Seeing her, would relent.
                              Hermes obliged, and leaving
The House of Heaven betook himself rapidly to the places
That are below the earth. He found King Death
At home in his halls, seated on a couch and by him
The girl, ashamed, hating his company and pining
To be with her mother (who, far off, was spoiling
The quiet lives of the gods). The Killer of Argus,
The unafraid Hermes, stood very close to Death
And said:
            'Hades, Black Lord of the Dead,
I am ordered by Zeus to bring Persephone
From Erebus, back among the gods so that
Her mother, seeing her, may cease being angry
And cease injuring us. She intends nothing less
Than the destruction of earth's humanity by imprisoning
The seed in the soil, and when they die, and that
Will not be long, where shall we unhappy gods
Get worship from? Her anger is terrible, she will not
Come near us but sits alone in in her temple
In Eleusis among the rocks.'
                              Thus Hermes. Unsmiling
Hades, King of Ghosts, smiled blackly

And bowed to Zeus, the stronger, and said:
'Persephone, go at once now home to your mother,
The goddess in mourning, and towards myself, if you can,
Be kinder, please, and do not think what has happened
The worst possible thing. You could do plenty worse
For a husband among the gods than me, brother
As I am of His Majesty. Down here
You will be queen of everything that has
Its being after the fashion of the dead and among
The gods none's status will be greater and whoever
Gives you less than your due and does not with offerings
Strive officiously for your favour and performs
Less than satisfactorily in your worship or
Falls behind in the payment of contributions he
Or she will writhe in Hell for ever.'
                                        Persephone,
The trusting, leapt to her feet full of joy
To be leaving Death but he, kissing her
Goodbye, slipped slyly from mouth to mouth
The juicy seed of a pomegranate so that
She swallowed it and was thwarted in her wish
Always to stay with her mother, revered Demeter
Cloaked in midnight blue.

                        Aidoneus,
Ruler of Many, Receiver of More and More,
Made a great show of harnessing his horses,
Undying among the dead, to the golden chariot
And handed his captive in. The Killer of Argus
Took up the reins and the whip and left the halls
Of Hell at a gallop. The enormous distances
Were put behind them in no time and over salt
And rivers of freshwater and lowland grass
And high crags they passed like a parting spear
Through the deep air.
                        Hermes, the coachman,
Reined the horses in, outside the scented temple,
The hiding-place of Queen Demeter. Like one of
The mad women of Dionysos when they career
Down mountainsides so Demeter when she saw
Persephone ran to her and she, the child,
Seeing her mother's face, the lovely, the beloved,

Jumped from the chariot, left the standing horses,
And ran and fell upon her mother's neck
Tight-hugging her. Demeter though, whilst yet
Holding her child again, felt suddenly cold
In the heart and her hands ceased caressing Persephone.
She cried: 'Oh, child, you did not, did you,
Tell me, taste any food underground? Say not
Or tell me the worst. For if you tasted nothing
Then you have seen the last of ugly Hades
Then you will live in the house of God your father,
Storm-brewer Zeus, the Castrator's son,
And me, honoured among the gods, but if
Down there you swallowed something you must
Go back into the lifeless places for one
Third part of every year's seasons
And stay with me for two. When with flowers
In spring, with the innumerable sweet flowers,
The earth revives, then you will surface again
Out of the dark, out of the mists, your coming will be
Wonderful to the gods in Heaven who see
Of springtimes an eternity and to men on earth
Who see a handful. But tell me, child,
How he took you into the dark who is the strong
Receiver of More and More, by what crooked means
Did he add you?'
                    The girl Persephone,
The radiant child, answered her mother thus:
'When lucky Hermes, the hurrying messenger, came
On the part of my father, the Son of Kronos, and the others
In Heaven, to fetch me from Erebus, that you
Might have me back again and relent in your anger
And hard grudge against the gods, I jumped
For joy. But Death, with a kiss, slyly
Planted in me the seed of a pomegranate,
Sweet to taste, and this I had to swallow
Though I did not want to.
                              And as to how
He took me in the first place with the connivance
Of my own father, the Usurper Zeus, and carried me to
That world below the roots, I will tell you exactly:
We were playing together in a lovely meadow, I
And the daughters of Ocean—these: Leucippe,

Phaeno, Electra, Ianthe, Melita,
Iache, Rhodea and Callirhoë,
Melobosis, Tyche and Ocyrhoë who is
Herself flowerlike, and Chryseis and Ianeira,
Acaste, Admete, Rhodope and Pluto,
Sweet Calypso, Urania and beautiful
Galaxaura. We were playing and picking
Armfuls of lovely flowers, such as
Irises and hyacinths, roses and more
Lilies than I have ever seen, but I
Loved most of all a certain narcissus,
Crocus-yellow at the centre, and when
I reached for this the earth, the broad earth
Full of flowers, gave and from that hole
The Lord who has Dominion over Millions,
Gold-chariot-driving, rose and took me
Under the earth into the dark, resistant,
Vanishing, screaming.
                              Mother, he sleeps and wakes
Where the dead are, their only light
Is like the pallor of tubers, he never smiles,
They never see the sun, and the worst is
That I have eaten what he gave me.'

                                        But all day then
Mother and daughter had an equal gladness.
They lessened for one another with embraces
The grief in their hearts, the loathing in their minds.
It was an equal giving and receiving
Of presents of happiness. Then Hecate,
Coiffed with the sickle moon, came near. She also
Hugged close the precious daughter of Demeter
And was her attendant and companion thereafter.

Thunderous God sent another messenger,
His mother Rhea of the Lovely Hair, to beg
Her daughter Demeter, cloaked in black, to join
The happy family of the gods again. This doing,
He promised, she would be given such honours
In Heaven as she thought fit. Her child, alas,
Must spend a third part of the revolving year
Below, in blackness, but the rest with her

In Heaven's sun. Thus God. And mother Rhea
Obeyed her bullying boy. Leaving Olympus
She hurried down to the Rharian plain which had
Once yielded goodness in abundance
Like an udder, but now nothing
And was idle and quite leafless, the white
Grain having been imprisoned by Demeter,
The proud walker, in her grudge. The place soon
After the coming of spring grew long-haired
With corn, the furrows filled, the binders
Bound fat sheaves. At Rharus then
Descending out of the unharvestable air
Rhea touched the earth and meeting her daughter
Both were happy. What roaring, big-eyed Zeus
Had told her to say, she said: that Demeter
Was to come home again to Heaven in return for
The promise of rights and privileges of her own choosing
It being understood that Persephone
Would live two thirds of the year in the light
And only one in Hell. Rhea the wife of
Father-castrating and child-swallowing Kronos
Urged upon her the wisdom of not provoking
Further that butcher's son.

                         'Give humankind
Quickly increase of the fruits of the earth
Without which they are starving.'

                         Crowned Demeter
Caused then at once the resurrection of the seed
In the ploughed ground so that the earth put on
A weight of leafing and flowering things. Moreover
She visited the just rulers Triptolemus
And Diocles the horsedriver and brave Eumolpus
And Celeus whom the people loved, and to Dolichus
And lastly Polyxeinus and to them all
She taught the conduct of her rites. She disclosed
Her mysteries by which we abide, into which
It is not proper to enquire and so holy that
Who thought to utter them the hand of the goddess
Commanding respect would stop his mouth. They are blessed
Those who on earth have seen her mysteries

But those who have not and had no part in them
They will be without any portion of that light
And peace when they die and go down to
Where darkness is and confusion.

                              Demeter,
When she had finished her teaching, re-entered
The circle of Olympian gods under
Loud Zeus. But on earth, where death is,
Those who are loved and favoured by Demeter,
The holy mother, and by Persephone,
Her radiant child, they will be blessed
With gold in the house and harvest and the heart.

Owner of sweet Eleusis and of Paros in
The sea and of rocky Antron, to whom we owe
The seasons, who weight the held skirts of our girls
With apples and fill the boys' embraces with sheaves,
O Lady Demeter look my way kindly, you
And your daughter Persephone who is
Beautiful beyond the reach of our praises, give me
Please a livelihood and joy at heart as I
Look your way, goddess, in song after song.

The Hymn to Aphrodite

These things are told by the Muse of golden
Aphrodite, the Cyprian, who excites desire even among
The gods, and men who are under death's dominion
Are under hers too as are the winged birds
And all creatures the land rears and the sea.
Garlanded Cytherea troubles them all.

Against three of her own kind it is true she is powerless:
Against clear-eyed Athene for one, the daughter of
Black Zeus. She is indifferent to love
And delights in discord and warfare, the works of Ares;
But also in the manufacturing of fine things.
She first taught earth's craftsmen the making
Of war-chariots in intricate bronze
And young girls the management of the house—all
Beautiful works of their hands come from her teaching.

Nor can the huntress Artemis, armed with golden
Arrows, ever be subjugated by Aphrodite,
The lover of laughter. For she loves archery,
The hounding to death of animals on mountains,
The clamour of pursuit in dark forests; but also
The lyre, dance and the rule of civil law.

Finally the virgin Hestia cares nothing for
The works of Aphrodite. Strangely born
The first and youngest child of cunning Kronos
She steadfastly refused Apollo and Poseidon
Who wanted her in marriage. On the head of Zeus
She swore to live her immortal life a virgin:
She had great honour from Zeus instead of marriage.
She has her place in the middle of the house,
The best portions are hers. In all the temples
She is reverenced. None of the immortals
Is more highly thought of by mortal men.

These Aphrodite cannot sway. Otherwise not one
Among the blessed gods nor any man
Has ever eluded her. She distracts the mind

Even of Zeus to whom the thunder is
A plaything and whose majesty is greatest.
She overcomes his wisdom whenever she likes
And easily brings him to bed with mortal women
Deceiving Hera his sister and his wife
The first in beauty among the immortal goddesses,
Born of Rhea and Kronos, the trustworthy
Consort of Zeus whose wisdom is endless.

And he caused Aphrodite herself to want
Union with a mortal man, for so long
As she remained innocent of human love
Among the immortals she could always point the finger
At their having been joined in love by her,
The laughter-loving Aphrodite, gods
With mortal women who bore them sons of death
And goddesses in love with mortal men.

He made her love Anchises, at that time
A herdsman on the steep slopes of Ida,
The mountain of innumerable streams, and like
A god in looks. She loved him immediately.
Desire took hold of smiling Aphrodite
As soon as she saw the man. She went to Cyprus,
To Paphos where her precinct and altar are,
Into her fragrant house. The shining doors
Being closed, she was bathed by the Charities
And anointed with an oil she had that the gods
Perfume themselves with. She clothed her body
In beautiful clothes and put on gold for ornament
And laughing she left fragrant Cyprus
And flew to Troy through the high clouds
Quickly making her way. So she came
To Ida of the innumerable streams
And mother of wild beasts and went at once
To the shieling across the mountain. After her,
Fawning upon her, came grey wolves and fierce lions,
Bears and the fast deer-hunting leopards.
It pleased her to see them and she made
Them lust, so that they coupled in the shadowy combes.

But she herself came to the hill farm

And found him alone there, his companions being out,
Anchises whose beauty was from the gods.
His companions were following the herds over the pastures
And he was quite alone in the house
Wandering here and there and strumming on a lyre.

Aphrodite, daughter of Zeus, she stood
Before him, like a virgin girl in appearance,
So that when he saw her he should not be afraid.
But still he was amazed, for she was tall and imposing.
He stared at her shining clothes. She wore
A peplos brighter than the brightness of fire,
Golden, beautifully worked, that shimmered
Like moonlight over her soft breasts, and this
Astounded him, and the twisted brooches, ear-rings
Like calyxes and, lovelier than anything he had ever seen,
Necklaces on her white throat. Then love
Took Anchises hold. He said: 'Welcome,
Lady, to my house, whichever one you are
Of the immortals, whether Artemis or Leto or
Golden Aphrodite or Themis or bright-eyed
Athene, or perhaps you are one of the Graces
Who are companions to the gods and are called immortal,
Or one of the Nymphs who inhabit the pleasant woods
Or one whose places are this lovely mountain
And where the rivers start and these grassy meadows.
I will make you an altar on a high peak
Where it may be seen for miles around and in all
Seasons offer sacrifices. You
Be kindly disposed and grant me eminence
Among the Trojans and strong sons for the future
And let me live long in the daylight
Prosperous among my people as I age.'

Aphrodite, the child of Zeus, replied:
'Anchises, second to none in fame among mortal men,
I am not a goddess, why did you think me one?
A mortal mother bore me to die as you will.
My father is Otreus, you will have heard of him,
He rules Phrygia with its many fortresses.
But I know your language as well as my own
For my nurse was a Trojan. She raised me

From infancy, in lieu of my dear mother.
Now Hermes, Killer of Argus, Bearer of
The Golden Wand, has snatched me from the dance
Of Artemis the Huntress with the golden arrows
Where we were playing together, nymphs
And marriageable girls and a crowd surrounding us.
Then Hermes snatched me from among them
And carried me over many tilled fields
And over much land owned by no-one and untilled
Where savage beasts stalk in the shadowy combes
Until I thought I should never again set foot
On the good earth. And he said I should be
The wife of Anchises and bear you beautiful children,
And having said so he, Hermes, withdrew
Among the deathless gods and I have come
To you, bound by necessity. By Zeus
I beg you now and by your noble parents –
For noble they must be to have a son like you –
Take me, a virgin and ignorant of love,
And show me to your father and mother
And to your brothers, that they may judge what sort
Of wife I shall make you, and send quickly
To the Phrygians, whose horses go like the wind,
To tell my father and my grieving mother,
And they will send you quantities of gold
And woven cloths. Accept these many gifts
As my dowry. Then let us be married since
We wish it and heaven and earth approve.'

Concluding, the goddess touched him to the heart
With love and desire for her. Anchises said:
'If you are mortal and born of a mortal woman
And Otreus, whom I have heard of, is your father
As you say, and you have come here by the will
Of Hermes, the Wayfarer, to be my wife
Lifelong, nobody human or divine
Shall keep me from lying with you here and now,
No, not if Apollo the Archer himself
Let fly arrows at me from his silver bow,
O Lady beautiful as a goddess, from your bed
I would not mind going down to Hades' house.
He took her hand. Then smiling Aphrodite

Averting her face and with her eyes cast down
Went slowly to the bed that was already laid
For the royal man with soft coverings, with
The skins of bears and of loud-roaring lions
Killed by him on the high mountains. And when
They were together on the bed he first
Removed the jewellery from her body,
Unfastened her dress at the shoulders, undid
The twisted broches, the ear-rings, the necklaces,
Loosed her belt and so one by one
Took off her shining clothes and laid them
Down on a silver-studded chair. Thus ignorant
Of what he did, by the will of the gods and fated,
He lay, a mortal man, with a deathless goddess.

But at the hour when the herdsmen drive the cattle
And sheep home into the fold from the flowery pastures
Aphrodite caused Anchises to sleep sweetly
But she dressed in her fine clothes again
And fully clothed stood by the bed tall
As the roof now and her face radiant with the beauty
Only the immortals have, and among them only Cytherea.

Then she woke him saying: 'Dardanus' son
I wonder what you are dreaming, look now
Whether I am as you first saw me.'
He heard her and woke at once, but when
He saw the throat and lovely eyes of Aphrodite
Then he was afraid and averted his eyes and hid
His face—that she found beautiful—in his cloak
Entreating her so: 'When I first saw you, goddess,
I knew you for what you are, though you denied it.
But now by implacable Zeus I beg you
Do not leave me like one of the dead among
The living. Have mercy. I know the very life
Leaves a mortal man who has slept with a goddess.'

Aphrodite, daughter of Zeus, replied:
'Anchises, best of men, be reassured
And on that score not too fearful. Nothing
Harmful will happen to you either from me
Or from the other gods. You will be loved.

You will have a son who will be dear to you and me.
He will be king among the Trojans, and children
Upon children will continue your family for ever.
He will be called Aeneas, on account of the grief
It gives me to have slept with a mortal man
Though among such your family has always
Approached nearest the immortal gods in looks.

Did not Zeus, despite his wisdom, carry off
Golden-haired Ganymedes for his beauty
To be among the immortals and pour them
Their drink, drawing the red nectar
From a golden bowl? They held him in honour
And wonder. Tros however was inconsolable
Not knowing where the whirlwind from heaven
Had carried his dear son whom day in, day out,
He mourned. Then Zeus took pity, and paid him
Compensation for the boy in the form of high-
Stepping horses—such as carry the immortals.
And with this gift Hermes, obeying Zeus,
Explained all and said the boy would neither
Die nor age but be like the gods. At this
Tros left off weeping and turned to rejoicing
And rode his stormy horses with a glad heart.

And Eos too, throned in gold, took up
Another of your race, Tithonus, also
In appearance like the deathless gods and asked
The cloudly son of Kronos that he should
Live for ever. Zeus assented. She had her wish,
Poor fool, who never thought to get him besides
Eternal life eternal youth and total
Remission of old age. Thus in the flower
Of his life he lived like one of the blessed
With the young and golden Eos by Ocean's
Streams at the world's end—until grey showed
In his hair and beard, marring their beauty. Then
Eos the Queen never came to his bed
But still kept him in her house and saw
To him with food and ambrosia and fine clothes until
Foul old age overwhelmed him and he
Was helpless to raise or move his limbs.

Then she thought best to lay him in a room
And to close the bright doors on him and there
He babbles on for ever and cannot lift
A finger, who was formerly lithe and strong.

I would not like you to be, after his fashion,
Not able to die among the deathless gods.
I should not like you for a husband in heaven when
Old age, common to all men, ruthless age,
The curse, the burden, that the gods shudder at,
Has enshrouded you. And even were you to live
Unaging and as you are now in looks
Still I should be ashamed eternally
Among the immortals because of you. For they
Were afraid of me who mated them all
By cunning with mortal men and women and laughed
At them and they were all subject to me.
But now who am I to speak having erred
Outrageously and taken leave of my senses
And got myself with child by a mortal man?

When he first sees the light of the sun let him
Be given into the care of the nymphs who inhabit
This great and holy mountain, for in nature
They are between mortals and gods. They live long
And eat heavenly food and dance the lovely
Dance with the gods and goddesses and with them
Sileni and Hermes himself, the sharp-eyed
Killer of Argus, go into the dark places
Of pleasant caves to lie down together in love.
And at their birth pines or high oaks spring up
With them on the nurturing earth, beautiful, tall
And flourishing trees on the high mountains. They
Are called holy places of the gods and no man
Would ever lop them with an axe. But when
The nymphs are fated to die and death is close
Then first those beautiful trees wither where they stand,
The bark dies on them, the twigs fall and the souls
Of the trees and of the nymphs leave the sunlight
Together. These nymphs will have the custody of my son
During his infancy, but when he begins his boyhood
Then, once, they will show him to you here. Later,

About the fifth year, I shall bring him to you again
And what I intend will be made clear.
He will be lovely then, he will be like
A god, and a joy to you. Bring him immediately
To windy Troy and remember if any ask
Who bore you such a son say this: that he
Was born of one of the flowerlike nymphs who inhabit
This wooded hill. But if, like a fool,
You boast of loving and lying with Cypris,
The crowned queen, Zeus in rage will blast you
With fire. Now I have said all I shall say.
Be warned. Never name me. Fear the gods.'

She rose then on the winds of heaven. Farewell
Goddess, Queen of well-built Cyprus,
With you I began, with you I shall continue.

David Constantine was born in 1944 in Salford, Lancashire. He read Modern Languages at Wadham College, Oxford, where he wrote a doctoral thesis on the work of the German poet Friedrich Hölderlin. In 1969 he became a lecturer in German at Durham University, and in 1981 took up his present post of Fellow in German at the Queen's College, Oxford; he is married, with two children. He is the English Literary Editor of the magazine *Argo*.

David Constantine's first collection *A Brightness to Cast Shadows* was published by Bloodaxe Books to wide acclaim in 1980. Bloodaxe also published a selection of his work in Neil Astley's anthology *Ten North-East Poets*. His *Talitha Cumi* sequence recently appeared in Noel Connor's poet-artist collaboration *Talitha Cumi* (Bloodaxe Books, 1983) with drawings by Barry Hirst. *Watching for Dolphins* is Constantine's second collection of poems.

His critical introduction to the poetry of Hölderlin will be published by Oxford University Press in 1984, and he is now translating a *Selected Poems* of Hölderlin for Bloodaxe. Also in 1984 his first novel *Davies* will appear from Bloodaxe, and his study *Early Travellers to Greece and the Hellenic Ideal* from Cambridge University Press.